Mary Todd
Lincoln

Joanne Mattern

ABDO
Publishing Company

visit us at
www.abdopublishing.com

Published by ABDO Publishing Company, 8000 West 78th Street, Edina, Minnesota 55439.
Copyright © 2008 by Abdo Consulting Group, Inc. International copyrights reserved in all
countries. No part of this book may be reproduced in any form without written permission from
the publisher. The Checkerboard Library™ is a trademark and logo of ABDO Publishing
Company.

Printed in the United States.

Cover Photo: Corbis
Interior Photos: AP Images p. 11; Corbis pp. 5, 7, 9, 15, 22, 24, 26; Getty Images pp. 18, 19, 23,
    25; Library of Congress pp. 20, 21; North Wind pp. 12, 13, 14, 17; Picture History pp. 10,
    14–15, 16, 27

Series Coordinator: BreAnn Rumsch
Editors: Megan M. Gunderson, BreAnn Rumsch
Art Direction & Cover Design: Neil Klinepier

Library of Congress Cataloging-in-Publication Data

Mattern, Joanne, 1963-
  Mary Todd Lincoln / Joanne Mattern.
      p. cm. -- (First ladies)
  Includes index.
  ISBN-13: 978-1-59928-797-3
  1. Lincoln, Mary Todd, 1818-1882--Juvenile literature. 2. Presidents' spouses--United States--
Biography--Juvenile literature. 3. Lincoln, Abraham, 1809-1865--Juvenile literature. I. Title.
  E457.25.L55M38 2008
  973.7092--dc22
  [B]
                                                                      2007009733

Contents

Mary Todd Lincoln

Mary Todd Lincoln was First Lady during a turbulent time in American history. Her husband, Abraham Lincoln, was the sixteenth president of the United States. The Lincolns lived in the White House from 1861 to 1865.

Mr. Lincoln was president during the American **Civil War**. This war tore apart the nation. It was a difficult time for the American people. The Civil War was hard on the Lincolns, too.

President Lincoln was very popular while in office. However, his wife was not as well liked. Many people did not agree with her actions and said terrible things about her.

Still, Mrs. Lincoln could be lively and fun. Unfortunately, she often faced sadness in her later years. She also suffered from mental illness. Today, Mrs. Lincoln remains one of the most tragic, yet courageous, First Ladies in American history.

Though excitable and often misunderstood, Mary Todd Lincoln was praised for always believing in her husband's abilities.

A Crowded House

On December 13, 1818, Mary Ann Todd was born in Lexington, Kentucky. Her mother's name was Eliza Parker Todd. Her father, Robert Smith Todd, was a banker. He also loved politics and held several public offices. His daughter Mary would come to love politics, too.

Mary's family was large. She had two older sisters, a younger sister, and two younger brothers. Mary's youngest brother, George, was born in 1825. Eliza got very sick and died a few hours after George was born. Six-year-old Mary missed her mother terribly.

Six months later, Robert married a woman named Betsey Humphreys. Soon, the family grew even larger. Mary and the other Todd children did not like their stepmother. Eliza had been quiet and sweet. But Betsey was outspoken and **strict**. She also favored her own children. For these reasons, Betsey and Mary often fought with each other.

As a result, Mary spent as much time as she could with her father. He taught her about politics and government. At that time, girls were not expected to know about these things. But Mary was different. She was curious and liked to speak her mind.

Mary's childhood home was an inn before her father purchased it.

Away from Home

Mary received an excellent education. In 1827, she began attending a school called Ward's Academy. There, Mary studied English, science, mathematics, and history. She learned to speak French and took dance lessons, too. As she grew older, Mary attended many dances, parties, and other social events. Everyone thought she was outgoing and fun to be around.

Mary graduated from Ward's Academy in 1832. Then, her father sent her to a boarding school called Madame Mentelle's School for Young Ladies. A French couple named Augustus and Charlotte Mentelle ran the school. It was less than two miles (3 km) from the Todd house, so Mary went home on weekends.

However, Mary preferred being at school. There, she felt peaceful and did well with her studies. She also became close to Madame Mentelle, who was like a mother to Mary. Still, she felt lonely much of the time. Mary later wrote that when she was a teenager, "friends were few."

Mary felt lonely throughout her life. She liked to wear beautiful gowns to make herself feel better.

Springfield

In 1837, Mary graduated from Mentelle's. That same year,

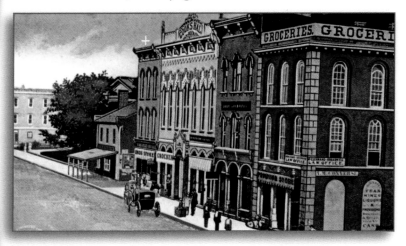

Springfield's streets were not paved in 1837. One muddy day, a determined Mary laid shingles down to get across the road!

Mary's older sister Elizabeth invited her to visit. Elizabeth lived in Springfield, Illinois, where she had married a man named Ninian Edwards. Their sister Frances was also living with the couple.

Mary made the trip from Lexington to Springfield by train and steamboat. She traveled for two long weeks. Springfield was new and **bustling**. There were many exciting activities for Mary to experience. She listened to speeches and attended dinner parties. Mary enjoyed her new independence. But her trip soon came to an end, and she returned to Lexington.

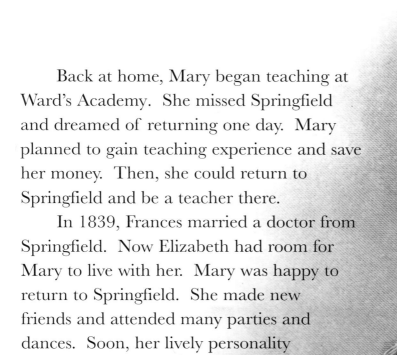

Back at home, Mary began teaching at Ward's Academy. She missed Springfield and dreamed of returning one day. Mary planned to gain teaching experience and save her money. Then, she could return to Springfield and be a teacher there.

In 1839, Frances married a doctor from Springfield. Now Elizabeth had room for Mary to live with her. Mary was happy to return to Springfield. She made new friends and attended many parties and dances. Soon, her lively personality made her one of the most popular young women in town.

Mary blossomed in her new home. She often spent hours exploring the streets of Springfield with her best friend, Mercy Levering.

Meeting Abraham

One night, a tall man approached Mary at a party. He told her he wanted to dance with her "in the worst way." Mary agreed to the dance. But the man was a terrible dancer and stepped on her feet! Afterward, Mary joked that he had truly danced with her "in the worst way."

That tall man was Abraham Lincoln. Abraham was 30 years old and ran a law practice in Springfield. He was also interested in politics. By the time Abraham met Mary, he had already been an Illinois state legislator for five years.

Mary and Abraham were very different from each other. Mary was outgoing. She was also used to fancy things and the prettiest clothing. Abraham was serious. He had grown up in a log cabin and did not care about his clothes. However, they both loved politics. And, they believed in the same things. By 1840, Mary and Abraham were in love.

Abraham only received one year's worth of schooling as a boy. As an adult, he taught himself many subjects, including law.

The parties Mary attended were very different from parties today. Dances had formal steps. And, ladies often carried a dance card to keep track of their dance partners for the evening.

A Stormy Romance

Mary's family did not approve of her romance with Abraham. They did not think he was good enough for her. But Mary did not care. She believed Abraham had a bright future. However, this did not prevent the couple from arguing.

Abraham's job required him to work long hours. One night, he was supposed to take Mary to a party. Abraham was late, so Mary left without him. She was so upset that she told Abraham she did not want to see him again.

Mary and Abraham did not talk for some time. This made them both feel sad and lonely. So in 1842, they began seeing

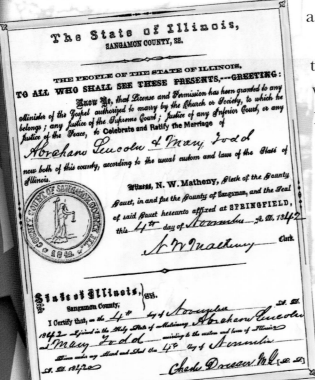

Mary and Abraham's marriage license

each other again. Suddenly on November 4, Mary announced that she and Abraham were getting married! They planned to marry in her sister Elizabeth's home. All the preparations were made that day. In fact, the wedding cake was still warm when it was served!

The **newlyweds** moved into a boardinghouse in Springfield. They paid eight dollars a week to rent a bedroom and eat meals in a dining room downstairs. Mary was often lonely while Abraham was working. And when he came home, she demanded his attention. The two fought frequently. Mary was not afraid to tell Abraham how she felt.

Mary was 13 inches (33 cm) shorter than Abraham! So, the couple only posed for a portrait when the artist agreed to downplay the height difference.

A New Life

On August 1, 1843, the Lincolns welcomed their first child. They named their son Robert Todd after Mrs. Lincoln's father. A few months later, the Lincolns bought a house in Springfield. The family finally had a home of their own!

In 1860, Washington, D.C., was not the same city it is today. However, the White House, the U.S. Capitol, and the Library of Congress had already been established.

The Lincolns did not stay in their new home for long. In 1846, they had a second son, Edward. That same year, Mr. Lincoln was elected to serve in the U.S. Congress. Mrs. Lincoln wanted the family to stay together. So they all moved to Washington, D.C., while Mr. Lincoln was working.

Mr. and Mrs. Lincoln's children brought them great joy. Sadly, little Eddie was often sick. On February 1, 1850, he died of **tuberculosis**. Mrs. Lincoln missed Eddie very much. But soon,

the family grew again. William, called Willie, was born later that year.
Then in 1853, Thomas was born. The Lincolns called him Tad.

In 1860, Mr. Lincoln ran for president. Mrs. Lincoln worked hard
on her husband's campaign. She wrote dozens of letters and
entertained important people in their Springfield home. When Mr.
Lincoln won the election, he ran home and said, "Mary, we are elected!"

During her husband's presidential campaign, Mrs. Lincoln
welcomed thousands of supportive visitors into their home.

A Nation Divided

Every year on July 3, the Battle of Gettysburg is reenacted in Gettysburg, Pennsylvania. It was one of the most important battles of the American Civil War.

When President Lincoln took office in 1861, the Northern and Southern states were fighting over slavery. The North, or the Union, said that slavery should be against the law. President Lincoln agreed. The South, or the Confederacy, said they had the right to make their own laws. That same year, most Southern states **seceded** to form their own nation. This began the American **Civil War**.

Mrs. Lincoln liked being First Lady. She enjoyed the power of her position. She also enjoyed being the center of Washington's social life. However, the **Civil War** made her life difficult. Many people did not like the Lincolns after the war began.

Northerners did not like Mrs. Lincoln because she was born in the South. Several of her brothers even fought for the Confederacy. Some Northerners believed she was a spy who gave Union secrets to the Confederates. Southerners did not like the president because he led the Union. And, they were angry that Mrs. Lincoln was loyal to her husband.

An 1861 editorial cartoon represents Mr. and Mrs. Lincoln arguing about the North and the South. Each is gripping half of a U.S. map. Born in the South but sympathetic to the North, Mrs. Lincoln was caught in the middle of the war's conflict.

Hard Times

Mrs. Lincoln had always enjoyed parties and fancy clothes. As First Lady, she continued to wear the latest fashions throughout the war. She also redecorated the White House and hosted large parties.

Many people became angry with the First Lady. They said it was wrong of her to spend money when so many people were suffering because of the war. President Lincoln tried to stop his wife's spending, but she fought back. Mrs. Lincoln insisted she get her way.

Mrs. Lincoln made many purchases as First Lady. Her receptions were especially expensive, despite the cost of the war.

Still, the First Lady wanted to help others. She visited wounded soldiers several times a week. She read to them, brought them meals, and wrote letters for them. Mrs. Lincoln also worked with the Contraband Relief Association. This group raised money to help recently freed slaves start new lives. Mrs. Lincoln was also the first First Lady to invite African Americans to the White House as guests.

Throughout her husband's presidency, Mrs. Lincoln's life remained difficult. In February 1862, Willie and Tad became sick with **typhoid fever**. Tad recovered, but tragically, Willie died. He was only 11 years old.

Willie's death filled his mother with grief. She even went to **spiritualists** to try talking with her late sons. Many Americans were upset by Mrs. Lincoln's new beliefs, but she did not care. She could only think of her sons.

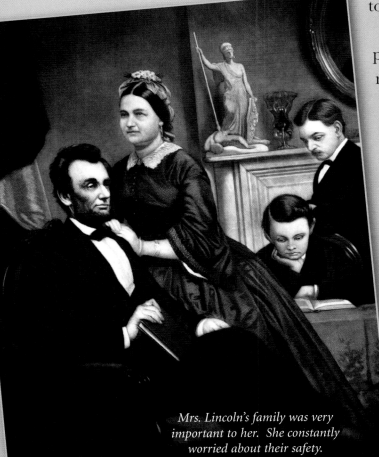

Mrs. Lincoln's family was very important to her. She constantly worried about their safety.

Ford's Theatre

After the assassination, Ford's Theatre closed until 1968. Today, visitors can attend plays as well as see the preserved theater box where the Lincolns sat.

President Lincoln was reelected in 1864. The following April, the Union won the **Civil War**. Mr. and Mrs. Lincoln were relieved. They hoped that peace would bring happiness to the nation. Yet, Mrs. Lincoln worried that something terrible would happen to her husband. She'd had several dreams that he would not live much longer.

On April 14, 1865, the Lincolns went to see a play at Ford's Theatre in Washington, D.C. They sat in a special box reserved for the president. Suddenly, a Southerner named John Wilkes Booth entered the box.

He shot the president, jumped down from the box, and ran out of the theater. Booth was eventually captured and killed on April 26.

President Lincoln was carried to a nearby boardinghouse. Mrs. Lincoln followed, crying and begging her husband to speak to her. But the president died the next morning. For many weeks, Mrs. Lincoln was too upset to go out in public. The nation mourned President Lincoln's death, too. He was the first U.S. president to be **assassinated**.

When John Wilkes Booth jumped from the theater box, he broke his leg. Still, he managed to escape to Virginia.

Conspiracy!

Most Americans know about the tragedy of Abraham Lincoln's assassination. However, few people know that his death was the result of a larger plot. The Civil War had just ended, and the United States was in turmoil. The U.S. government faced the challenge of uniting a bitterly divided country. The Southern states were angry about losing the war and blamed President Lincoln for their troubles.

John Wilkes Booth was a Southern man who sympathized with the Confederacy. He originally planned to kidnap the president and trade him for Confederate prisoners of war. However, that plot failed. So several days later, Booth shot President Lincoln and fled the scene. He was later caught and killed. Eight of Booth's conspirators were captured and put on trial.

Soon, the government learned that this group had wanted to overthrow the U.S. government! In addition to President Lincoln, they had intended to assassinate Vice President Andrew Johnson, Secretary of State William Seward, and General Ulysses S. Grant. They believed this would weaken the Union and allow the Confederacy to remain independent. Fortunately, no other assassination attempts were successful. And, the country eventually united peacefully.

Scared and Alone

Mrs. Lincoln did not know what to do after her husband died. She could not stay in the White House. And, she owed money to many people. Mrs. Lincoln worried because she knew she could not pay back the money.

Mrs. Lincoln's oldest son, Robert, had become a lawyer in Chicago, Illinois. So, Mrs. Lincoln and her son Tad moved there to be near Robert. Mrs. Lincoln also asked Congress to give her money to live on. Eventually, Congress agreed to a **pension**, but Mrs. Lincoln still worried. She decided to sell her fancy clothes to make money. However, people did not want to buy her used things. Instead, the public criticized Mrs. Lincoln even more.

In 1868, Mrs. Lincoln left the United States. For several years, she and Tad

Robert followed in his father's footsteps and became a lawyer.

traveled around Germany, England, Scotland, and Austria. Finally in 1870, Congress agreed to pay Mrs. Lincoln $3,000 a year. So, she decided it was time to return to America.

Then another tragedy struck. Tad became sick with **tuberculosis** on the trip home. Sadly, he died on July 15, 1871. Tad's death made Mrs. Lincoln more scared than ever. She began to think people wanted to hurt her. She worried Robert would die, too. Her fears caused her to have terrible headaches.

Mrs. Lincoln spent many years of her life wearing widow's weeds, the dark clothing required during periods of mourning.

A Sad Ending

Mrs. Lincoln continued to act strangely. Robert was worried and embarrassed by his mother's behavior. In May 1875, he arranged a trial for her. It took only ten minutes for the jury to declare Mrs. Lincoln **insane**. After the trial, she was sent to a state mental hospital. Mrs. Lincoln was upset and demanded another trial. In 1876, the jury said she was not insane. So she was set free.

For the next few years, Mrs. Lincoln traveled around the United States and Europe. Her health was beginning to fail. In fall 1880, she returned to her sister Elizabeth's home in Springfield. She died there of a **stroke** on July 16, 1882.

Mrs. Lincoln experienced many tragedies in her life. Yet, she was determined to face these hardships with dignity.

People did not understand why Mrs. Lincoln acted the way she did. In the end, she only wanted to feel safe and loved. Her husband had helped her feel happy, and she never stopped being loyal to him.

Mary Todd Lincoln was not always well regarded during her lifetime. But today, she is recognized as a strong, proud woman. She stood by her husband during one of the country's most challenging times. And, she has earned respect as a First Lady who was not afraid to speak her mind.

The first statue made of Abraham and Mary Todd Lincoln stands in Racine, Wisconsin.

Timeline

1818	Mary Ann Todd was born on December 13.
1827–1832	Mary attended Ward's Academy.
1832–1837	Mary attended Madame Mentelle's School for Young Ladies.
1842	Mary married Abraham Lincoln on November 4.
1843	The Lincolns' first son, Robert, was born.
1846	The Lincolns' son Edward, or Eddie, was born; Mr. Lincoln was elected to Congress.
1850	Eddie died of tuberculosis; the Lincolns' son William, or Willie, was born.
1853	The Lincolns' son Thomas, or Tad, was born.
1861–1865	Mrs. Lincoln acted as First Lady, while Mr. Lincoln served as president.
1862	Willie died of typhoid fever.
1865	President Lincoln was assassinated on April 14.
1870	Congress granted Mrs. Lincoln an annual pension.
1871	Tad died of tuberculosis.
1875	A jury declared Mrs. Lincoln insane at a trial in May; the following year, a second hearing reversed the court's ruling.
1882	Mrs. Lincoln died of a stroke on July 16.

Did You Know?

As a young girl, Mary often played pranks on her stepmother. Sometimes, she put salt in Betsey's coffee instead of sugar!

Including her stepbrothers and stepsisters, Mary grew up with 13 siblings! She had eight sisters and five brothers.

The term "First Lady" was not used by the newspapers until 1863. Therefore, Mrs. Lincoln was the first president's wife to be called "First Lady" while her husband was in office.

Mrs. Lincoln was very involved in her husband's presidency. So, the White House staff sometimes called her "Mrs. President" or "Madame President."

Mrs. Lincoln loved the French language. In fact, she often impressed her White House guests by having conversations with them entirely in French.

The Mary Todd Lincoln House was the first historic site to be restored in honor of a First Lady.

The Lincoln Bedroom is the only room in the White House dedicated to a president. Many important items from the Lincoln presidency are on display there, including a portrait of Mrs. Lincoln.

Glossary

assassinate - to murder a very important person, usually for political reasons.

bustling - noisy, energetic, and full of activity.

civil war - a war between groups in the same country. The United States of America and the Confederate States of America fought a civil war from 1861 to 1865.

insane - showing symptoms of a disturbed, or unsound, state of mind.

newlywed - a person who just married.

pension - a sum of money paid regularly by the government to former presidents or their surviving dependents.

secede - to break away from a group.

spiritualist - a person who believes that spirits of the dead can communicate with the living.

strict - demanding others to follow rules or regulations in a rigid, exact manner.

stroke - a sudden loss of consciousness, sensation, and voluntary motion. This attack of paralysis is caused by a rupture to a blood vessel of the brain, often caused by a blood clot.

tuberculosis - a disease that attacks the lungs, causing fever, coughing, and difficulty breathing.

typhoid fever - a disease that causes fever, headache, and intestinal inflammation.

Web Sites

To learn more about Mary Todd Lincoln, visit ABDO Publishing Company on the World Wide Web at **www.abdopublishing.com**. Web sites about Mary Todd Lincoln are featured on our Book Links page. These links are routinely monitored and updated to provide the most current information available.

Index